Raspberry Pi 4 For Beginners And Intermediates

A Comprehensive Guide for Beginner and Intermediates to Master the New Raspberry Pi 4 and Set up Innovative Projects

Craig Berg

Introduction

Thanks to its feature-rich nature, the Raspberry Pi is now one of the most used pieces of technology in fields such as scientific engineering, space travel, communication, 3D modeling and virtual reality, gaming, programming, and Medicine and Health.

Its adoption as a daily-use, standard desktop computer has also risen significantly even though the Raspberry Pi remains a tool favored mainly by hackers and 'techies.'

In this book, we are going to show you how to set up the latest model of the Raspberry Pi series, Raspberry *Pi 4*. Among other things, we are going to discuss:

- *The various Pi's available, which will help you know which Raspberry Pi to buy based on the features and functionalities you want as you buy one*

- *How to set up an operating system on the Pi and boot into the complete desktop mode*

- *How to work with the Linux operating system, which is the best operating system for the Raspberry Pi*

- *How to set up various programming environments on the Raspberry so that you can work with computing languages such as Python and C++*

- *How to troubleshoot common Raspberry Pi problems and issues*

- *How to use the Raspberry Pi4 at the highest level possible and unlock its superuser abilities —as well as your ability to work with the Pi4 to set up innovative projects*

And so much, much more ...

After reading the content in this book, you should be able to use the Raspberry Pi to create cool projects of your own – all you need is a little imagination, a Raspberry Pi, and this book.

Welcome to the world of Raspberry Pi, and let's get started!

PS: I'd like your feedback. If you are happy with this book, please leave a review on Amazon.

Please leave a review for this book on Amazon by visiting the page below:

https://amzn.to/2VMR5qr

Your Gift

Let me help you master this and other programming stuff quickly.

Visit

https://bit.ly/codetutorials

To Find Out More

Table of Content

Section 1

Raspberry Pi 101

Introduction &

Hardware

Configuration

Welcome to the World of Raspberry Pi!

The Raspberry Pi is a full-fledged series of single-board microcomputers developed and maintained by the Raspberry Foundation.

First created in 2012, the Raspberry Pi has evolved well over the years such that it now has illustrious capabilities and peripherals. The Raspberry foundation notes that today, they —and third parties— have sold more than 25 million Raspberry pi kits all over the world.

Let us take a look at the device's hardware composition.

Hardware Configuration

One of the Raspberry Pi's best features is its flexibility. You can buy a Raspberry Pi kit that comes equipped with complete hardware components and the Operating system to run it.

NOTE: It is important to note that like the Raspberry Pi, the hardware components that drive the Pi have developed well over the years with each Pi model having features that differ with that of its predecessors.

In this section, we are going to focus only on the latest model of the Raspberry Pi, the Raspberry Pi 4 released in June 2019.

The Raspberry Pi 4 CPU

Although significant changes have happened with each new release of the Raspberry Pi, all models feature a Broadcom System on Chip (Soc) with an ARM-compatible CPU. The Pi has a clock speed that ranges from 700 MHz to 1.5 GHz on the Raspberry Pi 4.

The Raspberry Pi 4 has a quad-core ARM Cortex-A72 processor, which is a successor to the Raspberry Pi 3 B+ processor quad-core Broadcom BCM2837BO that had a clock speed of 1.4GHz. Raspberry Pi processors support overclocking at boot by running the command sudo raspi-config during the boot process on Raspbian Linux based distributions. Most of these processors being overclock-able up to 800MHz and 1000 MHz and 1500 MHz on extreme edges.

Raspberry Pi Memory

The Raspberry Pi Foundation has done a great job of improving the device's memory. Older models of the device featured 128MB allocated for the GPU, with another 128MB allocated to the CPU. The GPU in Raspberry Pi is the Broadcom Video-core VI. The Raspberry Pi 4 comes in flavors of 1GB, 2GB, and 4GB.

Raspberry Pi Networking

Older models of the Raspberry Pi have no ethernet connectivity, and the only way to connect them to the internet is by using external USB ethernet or a USB wireless adapter.

Newer models such as Raspberry pi B and B+ support gigabit ethernet and use it as the primary interface for connectivity. The latest models of the Raspberry like the Raspberry Pi 4 also features an 802.11ac wireless interface and a BLE 5.0 Bluetooth. The Pi 4 also has Gigabit ethernet.

Raspberry Pi Storage

The default storage for the Raspberry Pi is a micro SD card. This SD card is what you will use to install the Operating system and as the default storage disk. However, it does support external storage devices via USB ports.

Those are the main features of the general Raspberry Pi. We may have left out some features that are specific to the Raspberry Pi 4 —instead of the entire Raspberry family— and that we shall now cover.

Hardware Specifics for the Raspberry Pi 4

As we have seen, the Raspberry Pi is a British-built, low-cost single-board computer that gives everyone the ability to learn computing, hacking, and programming with a lot of ease.

The Raspberry Pi 4 is a small device whose size is similar to that of a credit card or driver's license, but unlike a regular credit card, the Pi is a full-fledged computer that can run full operating systems.

Because of its flexibility, the Pi 4 gives you the ability to customize it by choosing an operating system of choice and the applications running on the device.

Setting up the Raspberry Pi is simple but can seem daunting to complete beginners. In this book, we will cover the entire set up of the Raspberry Pi from unboxing to using it to hack other systems.

Below is an image of the Raspberry Pi 4 with the exclusive features pointed out below.

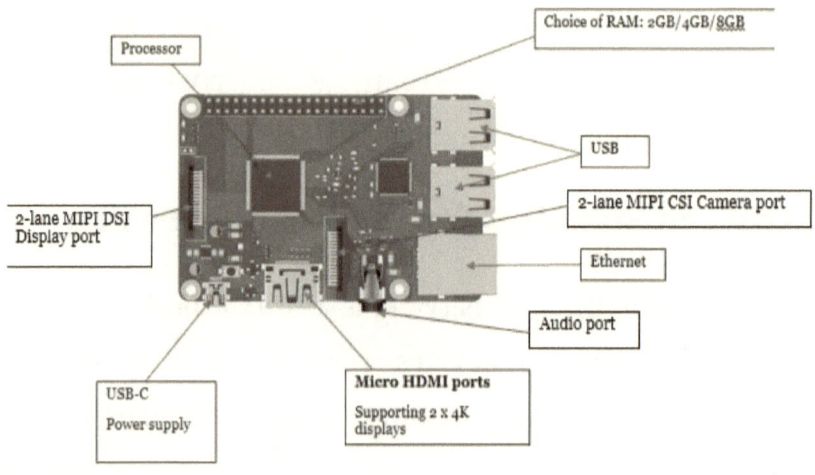

[1]Figure 1 Image Credit Shutterstock

Here are the purposes of each of these features:

- **The 40 Pin General Purpose** Input/output (GPIO) header connects projects with electric devices. You can access them directly on the Raspberry Pi.

NOTE: It is possible to turn some of the Pins on or off while your Pi is still running —or in operation.

- **PoE Header:** Power Over Ethernet (PoE) allows the device, once networked, to be automatically turned on/off at specific times. Raspberry Pi 4 features the 4-PIN header which supports the PoE HAT released on the previous model of Raspberry Pi 3B+

- **Gigabit Ethernet:** The Gigabit Ethernet hard built into the Raspberry Pi 4 features a bandwidth speed of over 350Mbps. Although this may not be as powerful as the regular desktop, it is a significant improvement over the Pi 3B+ that featured the gigabit Ethernet over USB 2.0 at 300Mbps. The Ethernet improvements add to the Raspberry Pi 4 feature-rich arsenal 4.

- **USB:** The Raspberry Pi 4 has 4 USB ports. 2 USB 2.0 ports and 2 USB 3.0 ports indicated by blue connectors. Since the Raspberry Pi 4 features built-in Wireless and Bluetooth, the possibility of requiring more ports is minimal since the required peripherals are a keyboard, mouse, and should you choose to add one, a webcam.

- **4-pole stereo audio/video jack:** The Raspberry Pi 4 has a 4-pole stereo audio and composite video port used to connect headphones or external speakers.

- **2-Lane MIPI CSI Camera Port:** The Mobile Industry Processor Interface (MIPI) Camera Serial Interface gives you the ability to attach an official Raspberry Pi Camera Module to the motherboard directly.

- **2-Micro HDMI Ports:** The Raspberry Pi 4 also has 2 micro HDMI ports that allow you to connect the Raspberry Pi to Modern Monitors. The ports support both audio and video with 4kp60 or 4K resolution support. These two Micro HDMI ports have replaced the full-sized HDMI port in the previous generations.

- **USB-C Power Port 5V/3A:** The Raspberry Pi 4 has a standard USB Power supply used to power the Raspberry

Pi. The Raspberry Foundation recommends using the Official power supply for the Raspberry Pi to avoid voltage and power issues that may damage the device. Like most single board computers, the Raspberry Pi supports 5v or 3 Amperes power input. The Power supply in Raspberry Pi 4 has changed to USB-C from a Micro USB jack available in previous models.

- **2-Lane MIDI DSI display ports**: The MIDI Display Interface port gives you the ability to connect a display directly to the Raspberry Pi.

- **Micro SD Slot:** Like older Pis, the Raspberry Pi 4 has an SD Card slot that acts as the hard drive for the board.

- **2.4/5GHzWireless and Bluetooth 5.0:** The Raspberry Pi 4 has a dual-band 2.4 and 5.0 GHz IEEE 802.1/* wireless connectivity and a Bluetooth 5.0 and LE. The wireless connectivity update makes the Pi 4 better than older models —in terms of connectivity.

The above are the essential Raspberry Pi 4 features you should be aware of; with these features looked at, we can now move on to discussing how to set up the Raspberry Pi 4.

Section 2

Raspberry Setup

How to Set Up Your

Raspberry Pi 4

In this section, we are going to cover how to set up the Raspberry Pi 4 and look at how to connect the devices that will ensure your Pi 4 runs as efficiently as possible.

Basic Requirements

The Raspberry Pi is just a motherboard; therefore, to use it, you need additions such as keyboards and other peripherals.

In most cases, the peripherals you need are easy to purchase and if you are tech-savvy, you may even have some of them lying around. The following is a list of essential items you need to use the Raspberry pi.

- Keyboard

- Mouse

- Micro-HDMI for Raspberry Pi 4

- Micro SD Card

The most important thing you need is a Micro SD card. Micro SDs are the types of SD cards available in and used by most Digital Cameras. If you are setting up an older model of the Pi, you may need to use a Larger SD card.

Once you have your Micro SD card, plug it in the SD Card slot. In Raspberry Pi 4, you only need to push the SD card and pull it out to remove it. On Certain Models, you need to push to insert and eject the SD card. Most SD cards provide a notch on one side to ensure that you insert the card correctly. Unless the Pi you bought came with an SD card that has NOOBS pre-installed, using your Pi will require that you install the software —we shall look at how to do that effectively.

²Figure 2 Image Credit Shutterstock

The next step is to connect to a display. For Raspberry Pi 4, it can be a digital 4k monitor or any regular display device. For older models, you have to use the Large HDMI cable. Connect the HDMI to the Raspberry and the respective display monitor.

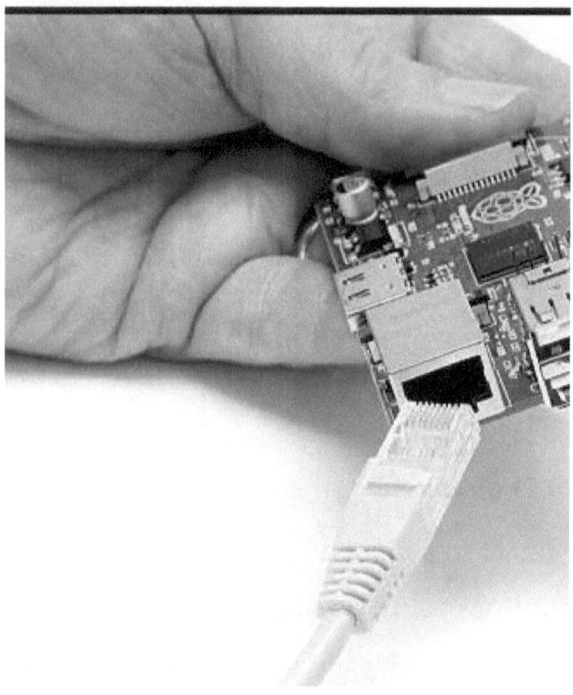

[3]Figure 3 Image Credit Gettyimages

The next phase involves getting your Raspberry Pi connected to the internet. You can do this by connecting to a cabled Ethernet connection or Wireless connection.

Since we have not booted up the Pi, it is best to stick with the Ethernet connection for now; later, we shall look at how to configure the wireless connection.

Connect one end of the Ethernet to the Raspberry Pi Gigabit Ethernet port and the other to your access point.

The next step is to connect the desired peripherals to the Raspberry Pi. As discussed, the Raspberry Pi 4 comes with 4 USB ports that support USB 2.0 and USB 3.0.

NOTE: If you are using older models of the Raspberry Pi, you may have to buy a USB hub so that you can have additional USB ports for your peripherals.

Connect the peripherals into the USB ports respectively. The Raspberry Pi comes with standard Bluetooth support and it is thus good practice to avoid plugging Bluetooth peripherals into your available USB slots.

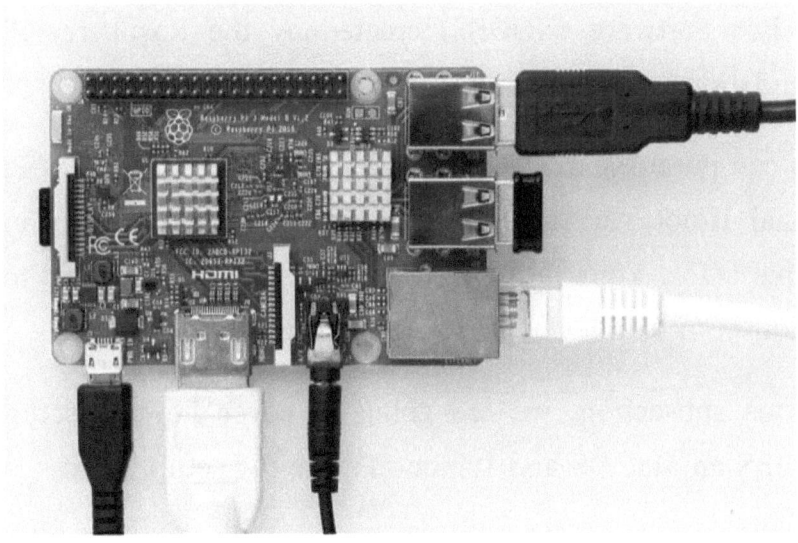

4Figure 4 Image Credit Shutterstock

Now that we have the peripherals connected, we can power up the Raspberry Pi. Connect the Micro USB cable to the power supply — make sure you use the manufacturer's power cable— and connect the other end to the 5v power adapter.

NOTE: Unless your SD Card has NOOBS installed, do not power on the Raspberry Pi yet. Instead, move on to the next subsection and learn how to configure and install NOOBS on your Pi 4 device:

How to Set Up NOOBS on Mac & Windows

Before proceeding further, we need to install the New Out of the Box Software (NOOBS) created by the Raspberry Pi Foundation for use in the Raspberry Pi.

You can purchase a NOOBS SD card from the Raspberry Pi official. If not, you can set it up using a personal SD card in simple steps. Your best bet is to use an unused SD or to backup your data if you are using an old SD card.

In this subsection, we are going to cover how to setup NOOBS on Mac OS and Windows since the setup process is similar.

Step 1

Download and install a Disk formatting utility. For this book, we shall use the SD formatter available here:

https://www.sdcard.org/downloads/formatter/

Once your computer completes downloading the formatting utility, open the installer downloaded and then follow the instructions to complete the installation.

Step 2

Ensure that you insert the SD card correctly into your Computer or Laptop SD Card slot.

Step 3

Open the SD card formatter tool and make sure that you select the correct SD card the 'Select Card Area.' Select the 'Overwrite Format' option to overwrite the data and Format your SD card.

You can also enter a name that allows you to identify the SD card; however, this is not necessary for installation.

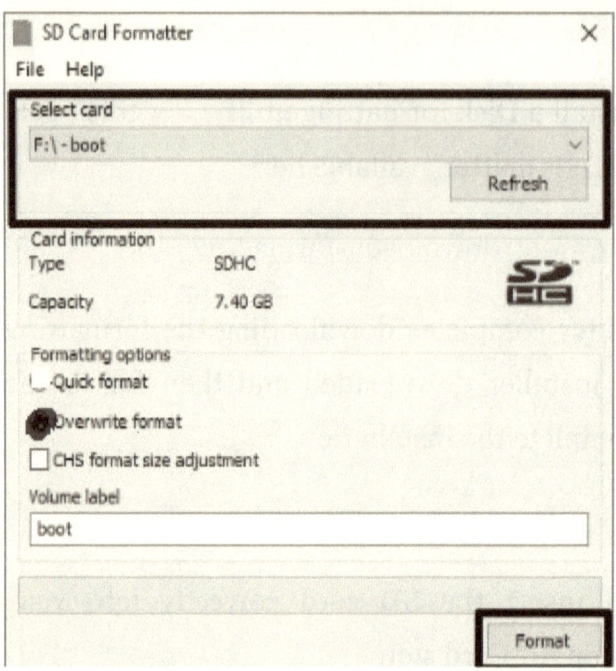

You can also use other formatting utilities such as the Diskpart in Windows or Disk utility for Mac. If you opt to use any other formatting utility tool, make sure that you format your SD card using the FAT32 format mode.

Step 4

Once the utility completes formatting, Mount the SD card and access it by Launching Finder or Explorer depending on your respective Operating System.

Step 5

The next step is to obtain a copy of the NOOBS software that contains Raspbian, LibreELEC, OSMC, Windows 10 IoT Core, Screenly OS, and such.

Navigate to the resource page below and select NOOBS, making sure to AVOID NOOBS Lite. Select your download method as ZIP or as Torrent.

https://www.raspberrypi.org/downloads/noobs/

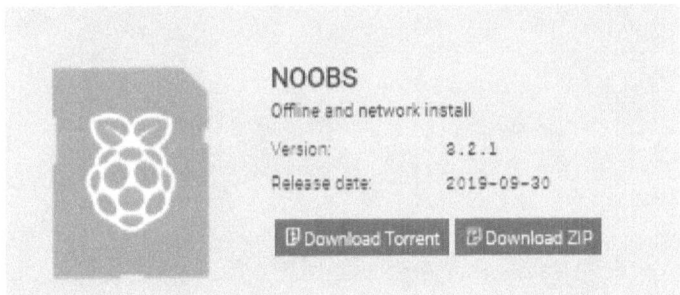

Step 6

Once the download is complete, open your computer's download folder and unzip the Noobs ZIP file. If you are using the default Zip manager for your operating system, click CTRL + A to select all the data available in the archive.

Once sure you have selected all the data, drag and drop all the files from the Archive to the root of the SD card. <u>DO NOT</u> copy these files into a folder within the SD card. Additionally, ensure you copy the files inside the archive and not the zip file.

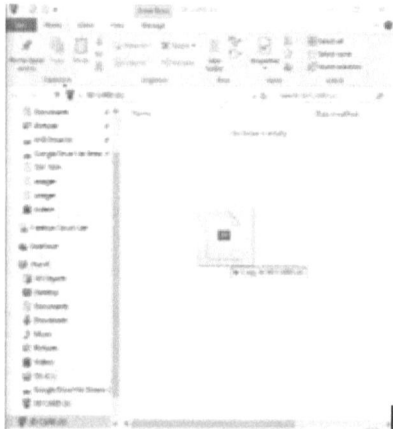

Eject the SD Card from the Computer and insert it into the Raspberry Pi. If you are setting up the Raspberry Pi on Linux, read the Linux setup section; otherwise, skip to the Installation section.

How to Set Up NOOBS on Linux

In this subsection, we are going to cover how to install NOOBS on Linux. We are going to use the terminal to perform the partitioning and extraction. This process may seem detailed and intimidating; nevertheless, work through it because it will be instrumental when using the Raspberry Pi to set up innovative projects.

For this guide, we shall use the latest version of Debian. However, any Linux distribution with the correct utilities installed will work fine.

Step 1

Launch the terminal and enter the command `sudo fdisk -l` to list all the connected disks and partitions in the operating system. Ensure to run the command as root or using an account with elevated privileges.

Step 2

The output will be something close to /dev/sda or /dev/sdb which indicates disk 1 and disk 2. If you have more than two drives connected, you may get /dev/sd(n) where n is the alphabetical number of the devices connected.

Step 3

Once you locate your SD card in the listed devices above, copy its identity code and proceed to the next step.

Step 4

The next step is to repartition and format the SD card using the FAT32 filesystem. Enter the command sudo fdisk /dev/sda replacing the /dev/sda with the code representing your SD card.

Step 5

Once you run the above command, you should see command m for help. Press enter to view all the commands available in the fdisk utility. We are only going to use the command d to delete all the partitions currently made on the SD card and command n to create a new partition.

Step 6

Now enter the command d and press enter. Enter 1 for the partition number. If there are other partitions in the SD card, enter command p to print them, then select enter command d and enter their corresponding partition number. Repeat this procedure until you delete all the partitions on your SD card.

Step 7

Once you are sure that you have deleted all the partitions, the next step is to create a new one so that you can install NOOBS. While still in fdisk, enter the command n and press Enter. Enter the command p to confirm the partition type as Primary and proceed. Now enter the partition number as 1 and click enter. Next, Enter the First and Last sector or press Enter to confirm the defaults.

Step 8

To confirm that the SD Card contains only one partition, enter the command p to list all the available partitions.

Step 9

To change the Filesystem from Linux to FAT32, enter the command L to list all the codes available. Once you locate the code corresponding to FAT32, enter it and click Enter. In this case, we shall select the t and b commands respectively. Once the operation is successful, the terminal shall display a message indicating that the partition has successfully changed to FAT32.

Step 10

Once you are sure the implementation of the changes is a success, enter the command **w** to write all the changes to the disk and confirm.

Step 11

Once we have finished creating the partition, we can format it by entering the command `sudo mkfs vfat /dev/sda/` where `dev/sda` represents the code for your SD card. These commands tell Linux to create a filesystem on the FAT32 partition of your SD card.

Step 12

Once the command has executed and successfully formatted the SD card, we need to download NOOBS, extract, and copy all the files into the SD card.

Step 13

You can download NOOBS by navigating to the resource page below. As mentioned earlier, make sure you select the latest Zip or Torrent download of NOOBS and not NOOBS Lite.

https://www.raspberrypi.org/downloads/noobs/

For this book, we shall use the Wget tool to download the file from the Linux terminal. Navigate to the folder you want to download the file to, for this case, the Downloads folder, by entering the command `cd ~/Downloads`.

Once in the download folder, enter the command

```
wget
https://downloads.raspberrypi.org/NOOBS/image
s/NOOBS-2019-09-30/NOOBS_v3_2_1.zip
```

Once you execute the command, wait for the download to complete.

Step 14

Once the download process completes, locate where the SD card is mounted by executing the command `sudo fdisk -l` and find the code. Now enter the command `sudo mount | grep -i sdb`.

Once mounted, navigate to the SD card by entering the command cd `/media/username/<device name>`

Step 15

Once in the SD Card root directory. Extract the files by executing the command `unzip ~/Downloads/NOOBS_v3_2_1.zip`.

This command will automatically extract all the necessary files into the SD card.

NOTE: You can complete the formatting process by using other utilities such as GParted. When using formatting utilities, take care not to Format Your System's directory.

With these steps done, we can move on to the next phase:

Section 3

Installing Raspbian

OS

How to Use NOOBS to

Install Raspbian

Once you have prepared the SD card and installed NOOBS on any operating system —Windows, Mac, or Linux—, you can begin the process that will help you install Raspbian OS on the Raspberry pi 4. Installing Raspbian OS will help you start using the Raspberry Pi as you would a regular computer.

As discussed in previous sections, make sure you have all the requirements, connect all your peripherals, and then power on the Raspberry Pi.

Once the Pi has booted up, a screen similar to the one shown below shall welcome you.

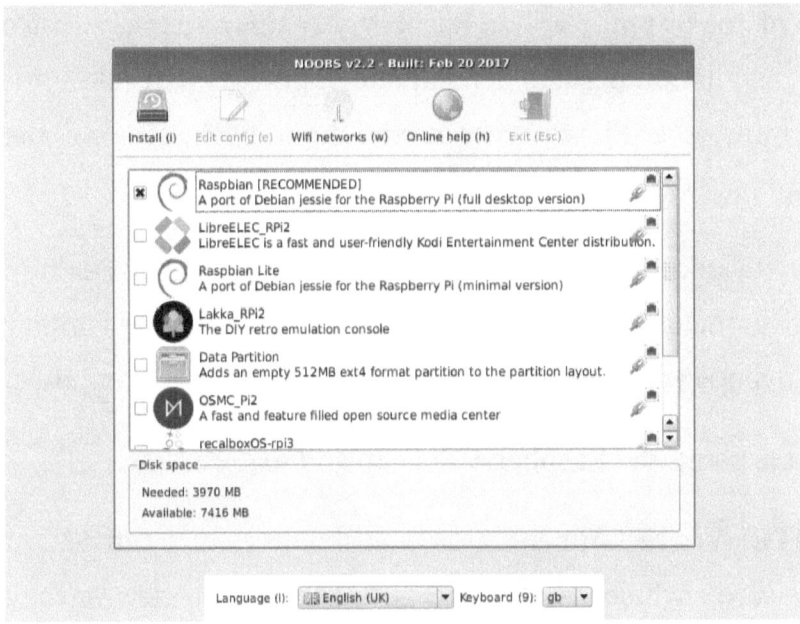

The welcome screen shall display a bunch of Operating Systems that you can install. Installing most of the other operating systems requires an active internet connection. For now, since our interest is the Raspbian OS, mark it and select the Keyboard setup at the bottom. Once you have completed, select the 'Install' option to begin the installation process.

NOOBS will now automatically extract the Raspbian file to the SD card, which will allow you to boot directly into Raspbian OS during the next bootup. During the installation process, the process is out of your control and all you have to do is wait for it to complete. You can use this time to grab a cup of Joe or read various Raspberry Pi tips and tricks. Once the installation process is complete, a process that takes 20-30 mins, the Pi will reboot and boot back up into the Raspbian OS.

The Raspberry Pi will boot directly into PIXEL Desktop Environment, a desktop environment that should be familiar to anybody who has used a Windows or Macintosh computer.

At this point, the Raspberry Pi is up and ready to use.

NOTE: As a recommendation, you should change the default password, which is "raspberry," and set a new strong password.

You can configure various options of the Raspberry Pi such as Language and Locale. The Raspberry Pi uses UK English as its default. If you are in a different location, you can change this by navigating to Applications ->Preferences ->Raspberry Pi Configuration ->Localizations.

If you feel more comfortable using the Command Line (CLI) than the PIXEL desktop, you can change the default boot options in the Configurations. For now, let us leave it as PIXEL a desktop.

To enhance your Pi knowledge, the next thing you need to know is:

How to Install Custom Images with Balena Etcher

In some instances, you may want to experiment with operating systems not included in NOOBS. Using custom images to set up the Raspberry Pi may seem complex —and it indeed is—, but in this section, we are going to discuss an effortless way to set up custom images. To do this, we are going to install Raspbian using the image rather than using NOOBS.

Step 1

The first step is to download a tool that helps you flash custom images to SD cards. Open your browser and navigate to the resource page below:

https://www.balena.io/etcher/

Select the version for your operating system and download it.

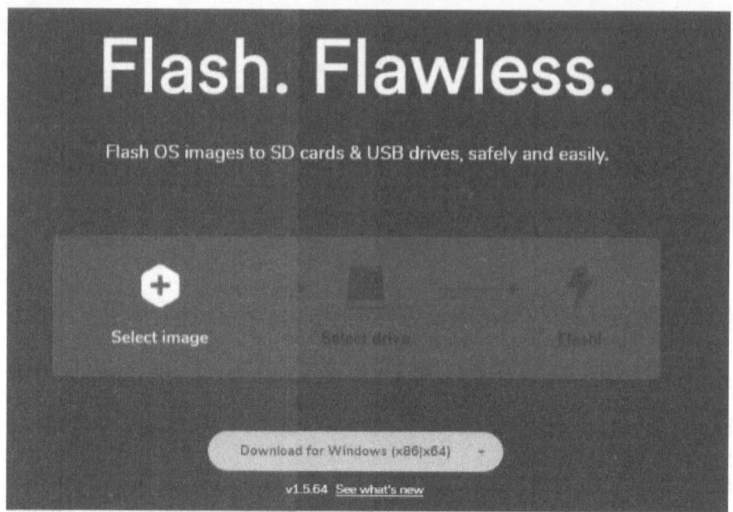

Step 2

Install the application you just downloaded. If you are using a Mac Os-based device, drag the file into Applications and Launch once done. Ensure that you insert the SD card you need to flash the image correctly into the machine.

Step 3

The Next step is to download the OS image you are going to use. Since we are setting up Raspbian OS, fire up your browser, navigate to the resource page below, and then select the Raspbian Buster with desktop and recommended software.

https://www.raspberrypi.org/downloads/raspbian/

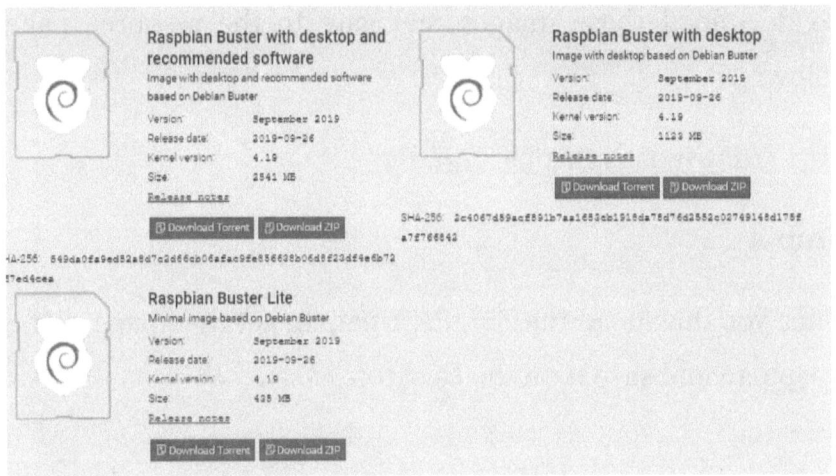

The Raspberry Pi supports various flavors of operating System —shown below— that you can install.

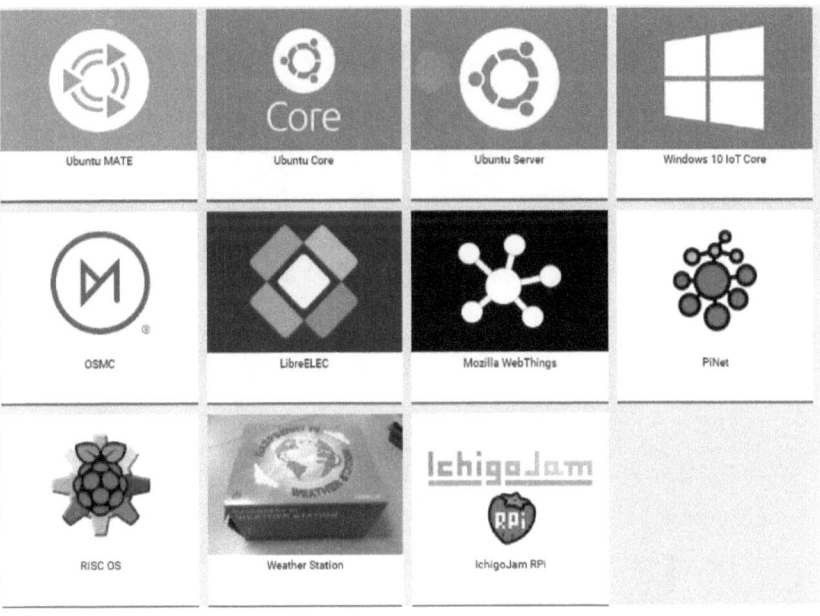

To download these images, navigate to the resource page below:

http://downloads.raspberrypi.org/

Step 4

Once you download the Zip file, Unzip to get the image of the Raspbian and save it on the Desktop.

Step 5

Once Etcher launches, it will show you an option that involves three stages namely image selection, device selection, and flashing.

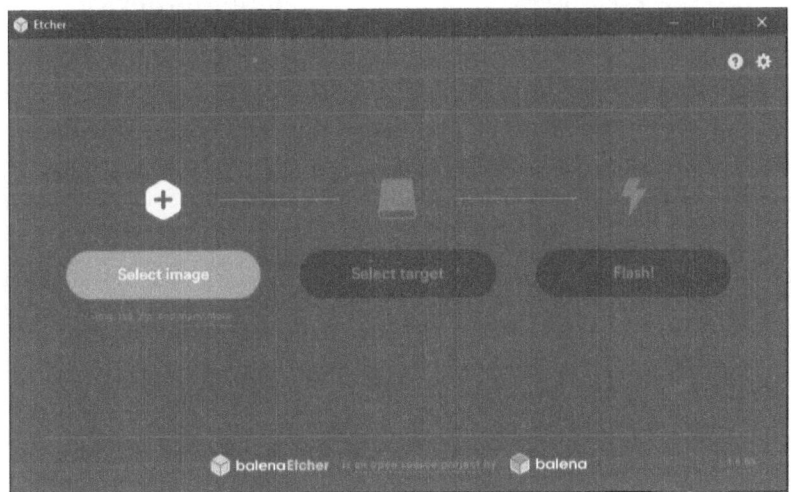

Step 6

In the select image section, select the Raspbian Image we just extracted.

Step 7

In the device selection section, select your SD card and mark it as the correct device to flash the image.

Step 8

Once done, select 'flash' to begin the flash process. The flash process may take up to 5 min based on your SD card's write speed. Wait for the process to complete, eject the SD Card, insert into the Raspberry Pi, and then boot up the device.

Setting up the Configuration File

Unlike a standard computer, the Raspberry Pi does not have a BIOS feature that you can use to control the boot process. Instead, it has a configuration file stored in the SD card and launched during the boot process, thus acting as the Raspberry Pi's BIOS.

The configuration file also helps flash the Raspberry Pi bootloader if any form of corruption occurs. The ability to control the boot parameters of the Raspberry Pi is useful when working with certain types of projects.

You can find the boot configuration file in `/boot/config.txt` in Linux distributions. On Windows and Mac, you can access it by navigating the folders of the SD Card. To edit the configuration file, you need root access; any changes that you make to the configuration file come into effect after rebooting the Raspberry Pi.

You must follow the correct format while editing the configuration file because incorrect edits might prevent the Raspberry Pi from booting. The right format for each entry in the configuration file is property=value. Each entry in the file takes up one line.

Newer models of the Raspberry Pi feature a # before the configuration file acting as disabled entries, which requires you to 'uncomment' them by removing the # symbol before the entry.

The following are examples of entries in the Raspberry Pi configuration file.

```
# Force the monitor to HDMI mode so that sound will be sent over HDMI cable
hdmi_drive=2
# Set monitor mode to DMT
hdmi_group=2
# Set monitor resolution to 1024x768 XGA 60Hz (HDMI_DMT_XGA_60)
hdmi_mode=16
# Make display smaller to stop text spilling off the screen
overscan_left=20
overscan_right=12
overscan_top=10
overscan_bottom=10
```

You can also view and modify the current settings in the configuration file by using the following commands.

- `vcgencmd get_config <config>` : We use this command to display a specific configuration value in the file.

- `vcgencmd get_config int` : We use this command to list all the integer configuration options that are true – meaning non-zero.

- `vcgencmd get_config str` : We use this command to list all the string configuration options that are true – meaning non-null

You can view most of the configuration settings by using the `vcgencmd` command. Other commands are unavailable when you use this command.

Configuration Settings

Here, we are going to discuss some of the necessary configuration edits you can tweak to make the Raspberry Pi more functional according to your needs. We shall categorize them into the sections Memory, Camera, Video/Display, Networking, Boot, Overclocking, and Audio.

Memory Configuration Edits

These are the most useful memory configuration edits for the Raspberry Pi. For newer models of the Raspberry Pi, uncomment the disabled entries by removing the # sign.

- `disable_l2cache` – We use this command to disable or enable ARM access to the GPU cache in the Raspberry Pi. We enable it by setting the value to 1; it requires a corresponding L2 disabled kernel. The default value may differ on various models such as those with standalone L2 cache.

- `gpu_mem` – Refers to the memory available from the GPU of the Raspberry Pi, including VPU, HVS, and other Legacy Codecs. We use this edit to set the memory split between the ARM and GPU of the Raspberry Pi. By default, the GPU memory is in megabytes. To avoid performance issues, always allocate the lowest possible value to allow the Linux system as much memory allocation as possible.

- `gpu_mem_256` : This is the GPU memory in Megabytes for the 256MB for the Raspberry Pi. The 512 MB Raspberry Pi usually ignores it, and the configuration overrides the gpu_mem. The max value for this entry is 192; by default, it does not have a set value.

- gpu_mem_512 : This configuration sets the GPU memory in megabytes for the 512 MB Raspberry Pi. The configuration becomes redundant and ignored if the memory size of the Raspberry Pi is not 512 MB. Likewise, it overrides the gpu_mem entry with a maximum value of 448 MB; the default value is unset.

- gpu_mem_1024 : We use this to set the GPU memory in Megabytes for the Raspberry Pi devices with 1024 MB of memory or more. If the memory of the Raspberry Pi is less than 1024 MB, the configuration is redundant and ignored. The gpu_mem_1024 has a maximum value of 944 MB with no default value set.

Camera Module Configuration Edits

Below are some of the Raspberry Pi camera module configuration settings. The camera module for the Raspberry Pi appears below:

[5]**Figure 5 Image Credit Shutterstock**

- `start_x` : We use this to enable the attached camera module in the Raspberry pi.

- `gpu_mem` : We use this configuration to set the minimum GPU memory for the Camera module.

- `disable_camera_led` : This configuration setting disables the camera LED from turning on when recording video or taking a picture.

Video/Display Configuration Edits

Here are the most common video configuration edits relating to video and display options for the Raspberry Pi. Once again, for the latest model of the Raspberry Pi, uncomment the entries to enable them.

NOTE: Because of the 4K support in Raspberry Pi 4 and 4B, some options may be unavailable in various models.

- `sdtv_mode` – This configuration defines the TV standard for composite video output. We set each mode by using integral values: 0, 1, 2, 3, 16 and 18, each representing: Normal NTSC, Japanese Version NTSC, Normal PAL, Brazillian PAL, Progressive scan NTSC, Progressive scan PAL respectively.

- `sdtv_disable_colorbust` : This configuration enables or disables color bust on the composite video output. Once you set the value to 1, it disables color outburst hence the picture appears sharper in monochrome.

- `sdtv_aspect` – This configuration defines the aspect ratio for the composite video output. The default integral value 1 represents the ratio 4:3. The integral value 2 represents the aspect ratio of 14:9, and the integral value 3 represents the aspect ratio of 16:9

- `enable_tvout` – This configuration enables composite output. Only the Raspberry Pi 4 supports this, which by default, disables composite output.

HDMI Options

These settings relate to the HDMI settings for the Raspberry Pi. Since Raspberry Pi 4 supports dual HDMI, you can tweak the settings for each HDMI as long as they do not conflict. You can do this by using the entry syntax: <command><hdmi port>

- `hdmi_safe` – We use this configuration to enable safe mode settings, which tries to boot the Raspberry Pi with maximum HDMI compatibility configuration. You can also achieve Maximum compatibility configuration by applying the following settings.

```
hdmi_force_hotplug=1
hdmi_ignore_edid=0xa5000080
config_hdmi_boost=4
hdmi_group=2
hdmi_mode=4
disable_overscan=0
overscan_left=24
overscan_right=24
overscan_top=24
overscan_bottom=24
```

- `hdmi_drive`: We use this to choose between HDMI and DVI modes.

- `hdmi_ignore_edid`: This configuration enables the option to ignore EDID/data for displays that do not have accurate Extended Display Identification Data (EDID).

- `hdmi_pixel_encoding`: Used to enforce the pixel encoding mode. By default, EDID requests pixel encoding, and changing the value is not necessary. The integral value 1 represent RGB Limited, 2 for RGB Full, 3 for YCbCr limited (16-235) and 4 for YCbCr full (0-255)

- `hdmi_force_hotplug`: Pretends that the HDMI hotplug signal is declared, so it appears that an HDMI display is attached.

- `confi_hdmi_boost`: Used to configure the signal strength for the default HDMI interface.

- `display_rotate`: Used to rotate the display clockwise on the enabled monitor. The integral values represent 90 degrees, 2 for 180, 3 for 270, the hexadecimal code 0x10000 for horizontal flip and 0x20000 for vertical flip.

- `hdmi_group` : used to define the HDMI type.

Hdmi-group	Result
0	Auto-detect from EDID
1	CEA
2	DMT

- `framebuffer_width`: Used to specify console frame buffer width in pixels, and is similar to `frambuffer_height`.

- `disable_touchscreen`: Used to enable or disable the touchscreen for the target display. The value 1 enables while 0 disables this option.

The Raspberry has very many Video and Display options that we cannot discuss here in their entirety. For more options, check the Raspberry Pi documentation that you can find on the resource page below:

https://raspberrypi.org/documentation/configuration/config-txt/video.md

Network Configuration Edits

The Network configuration is not very popular —the Raspberry Pi documentation may not have it. The following is the most common network configuration edit.

- `smsc95xx.macaddr` – We use this to configure the smsc95xx driver to use a random mac address on each boot instead of the default mac address.

Boot Configuration Edits

Here are the boot configuration edits for the Raspberry Pi. As usual, for newer models of the Raspberry Pi, uncomment the required entries by removing the # sign.

- `disable_commandline_tags` : We use this configuration to stop the start.elf from filling in ATAGS before kernel launch. The ATAGS is the memory before 0x100

- `Kernel` : We use this to set an alternative name while loading the kernel. The default name is `kernel.img`, `kernel7.img`, `kernel71.img` and is of type string.

- `Cmdline` : Used to set the command line parameters that can be used instead of `cmdline` text file.

- `disable_splash` : Used to enable or disable a splash screen on boot.

For some models, specific entries may be deprecated and obsolete. To find out more about boot options in the config.txt file, use the link provided below:

https://www.raspberrypi.org/documentation/configuration/config-txt/boot.md

Overclocking Configuration Edits

The following are the overclocking settings that you can enable on the Raspberry Pi. Overclocking has been allowed in Raspberry Pi models since 2012 without voiding the warranty. However, you should exercise caution to avoid overloading the processor.

NOTE: Setting any overclocking parameters to values other than those used by raspi-config may set a permanent bit within the SoC, making it possible to detect an overclocked Pi.

- arm_freq : Used to set the frequency of the ARM processor in MHz. The default value varies based on models such as 1000 MHz for Raspberry Pi Zero and Raspberry Pi W, 700 MHz for Raspberry Pi 1, 900 MHz for Raspberry Pi 2, 1200 MHz for Raspberry Pi

3, 1400 MHz for Raspberry Pi 3A+/3B+, and 1500 MHz for the Raspberry Pi 4.

- `gpu_freq` : Used to set: `core_freq, h264_freq, isp_freq, v3d_freq` altogether. The default value for this entry may also vary based on the specified model. For default values, check out the documentation on Overclocking available on the page below:

https://raspberrypi.org/documentation/configuration/config-txt/overclocking.md

- `core_freq` : Used to set the frequency of the GPU core processor in MHz. On certain models, especially those that came before Raspberry Pi 2, changing to this entry has a parallel impact on the ARM performance.

- `h264_freq` : Used to set the frequency of the hardware video block in MHz. It acts as an individual override on the gpu_freq entry.

- `isp_freq` : Used to set the frequency of the image sensor pipeline block.

- `v3d_freq` : Used to set the frequency of the 3D block in MHz.

- `avoid_pwm_pll` : It means not dedicate a pll to PWM audio. It may have a slight effect on analog audio.

- `sdram_freq` : Used to set the frequency of the Synchronous dynamic random-access memory in MHz.

- `force_turbo` : Used to enable or disable dynamic `cpufreq` driver and minimum settings.

- `over_voltage` : Used to adjust ARM/GPU voltage. The default value is 0, which equates to 1.2v.

- `Temp_limit` : Acts as overheating protection by setting the clocks and voltages to default when the SoC reaches the set value.

- `over_voltage_min` : Used to set the minimum value of over_voltage used for dynamic clocking.

- `sdram_freq_min` : Used to set the minimum value for `sdram_freq` used for dynamic clocking.

- `initial_turbo` : Enables turbo mode from boot from a given value in seconds (up to 60 seconds) or until `cpufreq` sets the frequency. To get more information on the initial turbo, check the resource below:

https://www.raspberrypi.org/forums/viewtopic.php?f=29&t =6201&start=425#p180099

Audio Configuration Edits

Here are the configuration edits used by the onboard audio output. These configurations mainly control how analog audio and firmware features enable or disabled on the Raspberry Pi.

- `disable_audio_dither` : Used to disable dither application.

- `enable_audio_dither` : Used to enable dither audio application.

- `pwm_sample_bits` : Used to adjust the bit depth of the onboard analog audio output.

You can find the documentation on audio configuration from the resource page below:

https://www.raspberrypi.org/documentation/configuration/config-txt/audio.md

NOTE: Other References for the Raspberry Pi configuration are available on the official Wiki:

https://elinux.org/RPiconfig/

That brings us to the end of this section. In the next one, we shall delve deeper into Raspbian OS

Section 4

Welcome to Raspbian OS

How to Navigate Raspbian OS Like a Pro

Raspbian OS is a Linux-based distribution used mainly by Raspberry Pi single-board computers. It comes prepacked with a collection of tools and apps that help you get the most out of the Raspberry Pi. It also supports development tools such as Python, Scratch, C++, and more, and office tools such as LibreOffice that is Microsoft Office compatible.

Raspbian OS also allows you to connect the Raspberry Pi to home and public networks using a cabled Ethernet or Wireless connection, which is only available on supported models. It also allows you to play music, video and other digital media. In later sections, we shall cover how to control the Raspberry Pi remotely from the Raspbian OS.

For now:

Introduction to the PIXEL Desktop Environment

PIXEL is a new desktop environment used by the Raspberry Pi and the Raspbian OS. It acts as the Windows and Mac GUI environment only fine-tuned towards Linux, programming, and electronics.

PIXEL is not that different from other Linux desktop environments such as GNOME, KDE, XFCE, LXDE, CINNAMON, or MATE, which is not very common on normal Linux distributions.

PIXEL, which stands for Pi Improved Xwindow Environment, Lightweight, is not a resource-demanding desktop environment, which is ideal for the Raspberry Pi.

The PIXEL desktop environment also features a more elegant and organization scheme than its predecessors. It has a fantastic graphical interface that makes using the Raspberry Pi easier than it would be were we to use the terminal window and the default interface.

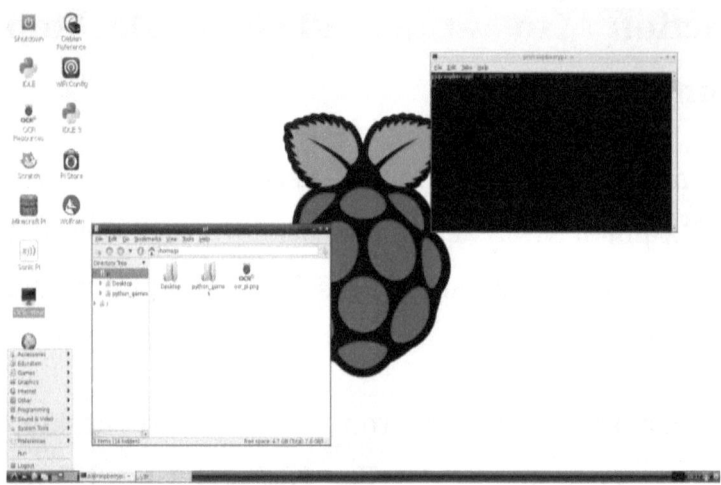

In this section, we are going to have a brief look at the PIXEL desktop environment and learn how to use it for the first time. If you are familiar with other Linux desktop environments, feel free to skip this section. If not, stick around.

Working with programs is straightforward because most of them offer graphical interfaces. To launch a program in PIXEL, click the left side at the top panel. Navigate to the program category and launch the program by clicking on it.

You can also edit the menu by removing or adding various applications in the menu. To edit the PIXEL menu, Launch the preferences applications and open the menu editor. You can add or remove apps by marking them on or off in the menu editor.

Once done working with the Raspberry Pi or switching users, you can shut down, reboot, or log out by selecting Menu –> Shutdown. Once you shut down the Raspberry Pi, wait for the screen to go blank before removing the power source.

You can also customize the PIXEL desktop by changing the icons, desktop wallpapers, and fonts. You can do this by navigating to Menu –> Preferences –> Appearances

The Raspberry Pi Command Line

If you've used Mac or Windows-based systems most of your life, you might be unfamiliar with working with the command line. For Linux users, this may be the only thing you use all day.

A command line or terminal is a window that sits between the desktop environment and the core part of the Operating System. The command line allows you to control the computer using text commands. Getting familiar with the command line is very important when using the Raspberry Pi.

To open the Terminal on the Raspberry Pi, navigate to Menu – terminal.

```
pi@raspberrypi:~ $ pwd
/home/pi
pi@raspberrypi:~ $ ls
pi@raspberrypi:~ $ mkdir NewFolder
pi@raspberrypi:~ $ ls
NewFolder
pi@raspberrypi:~ $ cd NewFolder
pi@raspberrypi:~/NewFolder $ cd ..
pi@raspberrypi:~ $ ls
NewFolder
pi@raspberrypi:~ $ cd NewFolder
pi@raspberrypi:~/NewFolder $ touch NewFile.txt
pi@raspberrypi:~/NewFolder $ ls
NewFile.txt
pi@raspberrypi:~/NewFolder $ cp NewFile.txt OtherFile.txt
pi@raspberrypi:~/NewFolder $ ls
NewFile.txt  OtherFile.txt
pi@raspberrypi:~/NewFolder $ rm NewFile.txt
pi@raspberrypi:~/NewFolder $ ls
OtherFile.txt
pi@raspberrypi:~/NewFolder $ mv OtherFile.txt /home/pi/
pi@raspberrypi:~/NewFolder $ cd ..
pi@raspberrypi:~ $ ls
NewFolder  OtherFile.txt
pi@raspberrypi:~ $ []
```

Linux Terminal Basics

The following are the command line basics for working with the Linux terminal. This section covers the overview; it does not get into detailed information. To get more familiar with Linux and the command line, check out a book geared more towards Linux.

The following commands are common when working with Linux.

- `mkdir` : Used to create a new directory inside the specified directory.

- `pwd` : Used to get the current working directory.

- `Sudo`: Used to perform the specified Linux command using superuser privileges.

- `Cp` : Used to copy files and directories from one source to the specified destination.

- `rm` : Used to remove the specified files and directories.

- `help` : Used to get help with a specified command.

- `man` : Used to get the manual documentation for the specified tool.

- `cd` : Used to change between directories with the Linux Filesystem

Connecting the Raspberry Pi

If you are using a cabled Ethernet connection, the Raspberry Pi will automatically connect to the internet. If you want to connect using a wireless connection, click on the network icon found at the top panel to view all the available networks.

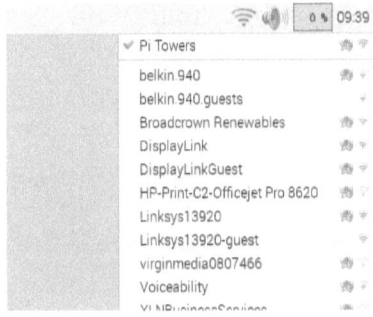

Once you locate a network you would like to connect to, select it and provide the password —if you are connecting to a secured network— and click OK to join that specific network.

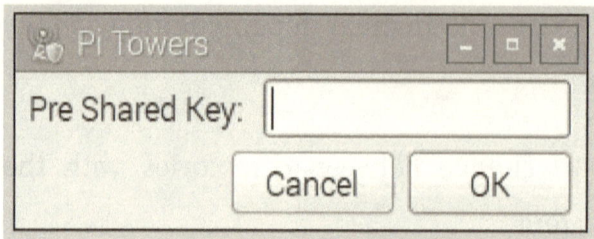

Once connected, you should see a Wi-Fi logo on the menu bar; that means you are now connected. To check the IP address of the Raspberry Pi, open the terminal and enter the command `ifconfig | grep more`

Setting Up Static IP

If you are on a busy network that has many devices connected to, it can be challenging to keep track of the Raspberry Pi IP address on each boot especially if you have connected to a network that is using DHCP. A static IP allows us to set one unique IP address that the Raspberry Pi will use, which helps with finding the Pi.

If you are unfamiliar with DHCP and IP addresses, here is an overview of how they work.

Once you connect a device to a network, the router/modem automatically assigns a unique number made up of four blocks of numbers known as Internet Protocol. The Internet

Protocol number is usually something similar to 192.168.0._
The first three blocks represent the network, and the third block represents the host —this depends on the network subnet mask. The last digit represents the device number.

When assigning IP addresses, the router takes the first three blocks representing the network and appends a digit to represent the connected host. The router itself is number 1 and you can find it at 192.168.0.1. For example, 192.168.0.2 may represent your desktop, 192.168.0.3 may represent your laptop, and 192.168.0.4 may represent your smartphone, etc.

NOTE: You can find the IP address of the Raspberry Pi by Opening the terminal and typing `ipconfig`.

This number may, however, vary based on the number of connected devices and their mode/nature of connection since the router is responsible for assigning this unique number. The router does this by using the Dynamic Host Configuration Protocol (DHCP), which means that it dynamically assigns IP addresses to the connected hosts. For example, if you disconnect the Raspberry Pi and connect other devices before reconnecting the Raspberry Pi, the Pi may get a different IP address once re-connected.

The implication of this is that you cannot memorize one IP address as the Raspberry Pi's until you configure it to use one unique IP, which is where static IP addresses come in handy. By using DHCP Reservation, we tell the router to remember this IP address for the Raspberry Pi only.

You can configure DHCP Reservation using the Router administration panel or edit the Raspberry Pi configurations. Since the routers' administrations may vary, we are going to look at how to work with the Raspberry Pi network configurations.

Step 1

The first step is to check whether DHCP service is running by executing the command `sudo service dhcp status`

Step 2

If DHCP is not running, execute the following commands consecutively:

```
sudo systemctl start dhcpd.service

sudo systemctl enable dhcpd
```

Step 3

Once the commands execute successfully, recheck whether DHCP is running and follow the next command

Step 4

Next, find the DHCP configuration file by executing the command `find dhcpcd.conf`

Step 5

Once you get the file location of the DHCP configuration file, edit it using the command line text editor Nano. Execute the following command.

```
sudo nano /etc/dhcpcd.conf
```

Step 6

If you have connected your Raspberry Pi via a cabled Ethernet, the interface is eth0 and wlan0 for Wifi connections.

Step 7

Enter the following lines in the Raspberry Pi DHCP configuration file.

```
interface eth0/wlan0

static ip_address=192.168.0.4/24

static routers=192.168.0.1

static domain_name_servers=1.1.1.1
```

The interface entry should contain the interface you have connected the Raspberry Pi to; for Ethernet, eth0, and wlan0 for Wireless.

NOTE: Use either eth0 or wlan0, not both

For static IP, set the desired IP address for the Raspberry Pi. The IP should not be an IP assigned to other devices on the same network. Additionally, the IP should be within the subnet range. For example, 192.168.0.2 – 192.168.0.254

Static routers should contain the IP address of the router. By default, this is 192.168.0.1. You can also specify the DNS servers you would like to use. If you do not know, set it to the IP address of the router; otherwise, specify it.

Step 8

Once done, press CTRL + X and click enter twice to save the configuration file. Now reboot the Pi by executing the command `sudo reboot`.

Step 9

Once rebooted, test the TCP/IP stack. Open the terminal and enter the command `ping raspberrypi.local`

```
$ ping raspberrypi.local

Pinging raspberrypi.local [192.168.137.72] with 32 bytes of data:
Reply from 192.168.137.72: bytes=32 time=1ms TTL=64
Reply from 192.168.137.72: bytes=32 time<1ms TTL=64
Reply from 192.168.137.72: bytes=32 time<1ms TTL=64
Reply from 192.168.137.72: bytes=32 time<1ms TTL=64

Ping statistics for 192.168.137.72:
    Packets: Sent = 4, Received = 4, Lost = 0 (0% loss),
Approximate round trip times in milli-seconds:
    Minimum = 0ms, Maximum = 1ms, Average = 0ms
```

As mentioned earlier, you can connect to the Raspberry Pi 4 remotely. The next section discusses how to do this effectively:

Section 5

Remote Connections

How to Work With the Raspberry Pi Remote Connection

One of the best ways of working with the Raspberry Pi is by accessing it remotely. Using SSH or VNC, you can connect to the Raspberry Pi remotely and work with it as if you were carrying it with you as if it were a laptop.

In this section, we are going to cover various methods of controlling the Raspberry Pi remotely.

How to Connect to the Pi Remotely Via VNC

Virtual Network Computing or VNC is a remote access technique that gives you remote control of one computer from another. The technology helps to communicate with servers and cloud computers from the basic Windows or Mac computer.

Since the Raspberry Pi does not feature a built-in monitor, it is best to control it by using a terminal or desktop environment from another computer. Here is how to do that:

Step 1

Setting up VNC may require terminal commands based on the distribution you are setting it in. For Raspberry Pi, the PIXEL desktop makes it very easy.

Step 2

To navigate to the Raspberry Pi VNC configuration, click on Menu –> Preferences –> Raspberry Pi Configuration –> Interfaces and enable VNC

Step 3

Once activated, a new icon marked VNC shall appear on the top-right menu bar. Click the icon to open the VNC server settings. Here, you will see a section labeled "Ready for Connections" and "Get Started" section. You can view the instructions by clicking on the arrow next to the "Get started section."

Step 4

Note the IP address the Raspberry Pi is using, which you can find under the "Get started" section. You can also use `ifconfig` to see the Raspberry Pi's IP address.

Step 5

Save the VNC server signature and catchphrase that contains a list of randomly generated words.

Step 5

Download and install a VNC viewer software that will enable you to control the Raspberry Pi. Ensure to install it on the device you wish to manage the Pi from and not the Raspberry Pi.

Visit the web page below to download Real VNC.

https://realvnc.com/download/viewer

Install the software on your device. It is compatible with any Operating System.

Step 6

Once installed, Launch VNC viewer and provide the IP address of the Raspberry Pi noted above. Under Encryption, select "Let VNC server choose" and click connect.

Step 7

Provide the username and password for the Raspberry Pi. If you are using default credentials, they are `username - pi, password - raspberry`.

Step 8

Ensure the catchphrase and the signature are valid to ensure you are connecting to the right device.

Step 9

Once connected, the VNC viewer will display the PIXEL desktop environment as if you were using the Raspberry Pi.

How to Connect to The Raspberry Pi Remotely Via SSH

Another way to connect to the Raspberry Pi remotely is via SSH. To connect the Raspberry Pi via SSH, open the terminal or Command prompt on Mac/Linux or Windows.

On the Raspberry Pi, use `ifconfig` to note down the IP address. On your computer's terminal, enter the command `ssh pi@192.168.0.8` where the pi is your Raspberry Pi's username, and the 192.168.0.8 is your Raspberry Pi's IP address. Once connected, enter the password for the pi username to connect. Unless you have configured SSH to run on a different port, the default port should work.

The next section looks at how to work with Advanced Packaging Tools (APT)

Section 6

Working with APT

Raspberry Pi uses Raspbian OS, which is a Debian based Linux distribution. That means that the Pi uses the APT package manager and has repositories similar to those of Debian. The Advanced Packaging Tools (APT) allows Debian-based users to install and update programs and libraries, which makes learning how to use APT critical to your ability to use the Raspberry Pi to set up innovative projects.

To update the repositories for the Raspberry Pi stored in /etc /apt/sources.list/, use the command, apt update

Installing programs using the APT command requires knowledge of the exact name of the program as stated in the repositories. For example, to install an IRC client called WeeChat, we can use the command, apt-get install weechat-curses -y

The first command apt-get calls the apt package manager. The second commands specify the action we want to carry out —in this case, install a software – followed by the package name. We use the y flag to set yes to all installation prompts.

We use the same command when removing programs. However, we replace the command install with remove.

Removing apps with apt does not remove the supporting files, and you, therefore, need to clean them using the commands `sudo apt purge <package name>`. To clean up the packages, you use the command `sudo apt clean`

To update the entire system and the packages available all at once, use the commands:

```
sudo apt-get update && sudo apt-get upgrade && sudo apt-get -dist-upgrade
```

To search for an app to install or remove, you can use the apt-cache command followed by the name of a similar program to install. For example, `apt-cache pkgnames | less`

To view all the installed packages, you can use the dpkg tool that acts similarly to the apt package manager. Use the command `sudo dpkg -get-selections | grep -v deinstall | less` to list all the packages installed on the Raspberry Pi.

NOTE: You need Root access when using the apt command, which means you need to use the command `sudo` before the `apt` command.

The next section will show you how to set up programming environments on the Raspberry Pi:

Section 7

How to Set Up Programming Environments on the Raspberry Pi

The Raspberry Pi is an essential programming tool. Thanks to its simplicity, it allows you to set up various programming environments fast.

In this section, we are going to look at how to set up programming environments for Python and C++ on the Raspberry.

NOTE: This is not a programming guide. As such, the book does not delve deep into how to write programs in the specified computer languages. To learn how to create computer programs in C++ and Python, check out my other books: https://bit.ly/codetutorials

How to Install Python 3 On the Raspberry Pi

Raspbian OS comes pre-installed with the latest, stable version of Python, which makes the Pi a swell python programming platform that you can use to script or work with for data science. Beginners also get a lot from the Raspberry Pi programming default setups since python is an excellent programming language.

You can launch the python IDLE shell by selecting Menu –> Programming –> Python IDLE. The Python on the Pi is the default Python package that does not contain additional libraries and packages.

If for some reason, you do not have the python shell, you can download the python installation package from the Python resource page below and select your desired version.

https://python.org/downloads

To test whether you have installed python correctly, open the terminal and enter the command: `python -version` to get the version of python installed.

C++ Installation

C++ is one of the most powerful programming languages used to create a wide range of applications. Programmers use it to create games, browsers, embedded systems, and Operating Systems.

This subsection looks at how you can start using c++ on Raspbian OS.

To check whether your Raspbian version has the C++ compiler installed, open the terminal and enter the command `whatis gcc`. If you do not have the compiller pre-installed, you can install it by executing the command `sudo apt-get update && sudo apt-get install gcc`

You can edit the code in nano or use the Geany editor pre-packaged in Raspbian. Navigate to Menu –> Programming –> Geany and edit the code.

NOTE: You can start learning how to program using free resources available online. Check the links below to get started.

http://www.cprogramming.com/

http://www.learn-c.org/

http://www.c4learn.com/

Section 8

Troubleshooting

Raspberry Pi

Troubleshooting

Since the Raspberry Pi is a full-fledged computer, you will encounter various problems that you will need to troubleshoot and fix.

The Raspberry Pi hardware and software are very stable and reliable; usually, the problems that occur have to do with setup and configuration errors than they are to do with hardware issues. However, we cannot altogether rule out hardware issues that you may need to fix.

In this section, we are going to cover the most common Raspberry Pi problems and how to fix them.

NOTE: Do not perform any operations on the Raspberry Pi board unless you are a certified engineer. Messing up the Raspberry Pi circuitry may damage the device irreparably and render the warranty void.

Red Power Blinking

If you notice a red blinking light on your Raspberry Pi, the chance are high that you have a power supply issue.

If the power supply is dropping out and supplying less than the required power current for the model you are using, it will cause the red blinking. To resolve this issue, you can use a different but recommended power supply.

Colored Splash Screen

A colored splash screen on the Raspberry Pi displays after you load the Raspberry Pi's GPU firmware (start.efl). However, when the splash screen displays, the Linux console automatically replaces it seconds later, which helps to troubleshoot and disable features that are causing problems.

The primary cause of this issue is an issue of a corrupted `kernel.img` that renders the device unable to complete the boot process. You can fix this problem by replacing the current kernel image with a compatible kernel image.

NOTE: Ensure to replace the current kernel image with a compatible one. You can find information on how to build one from the following resource page.

https://www.raspberrypi.org/documentation/linux/kernel/

Green LED blinks

On most occasions, the Raspberry Pi LED will start to blink green in particular patterns. It is essential to note the pattern so that you can determine the cause of the problem.

The following are the noticeable patterns and their associated issues.

- **1 Flash:** This problem is a result of SD card issues and failed boot device. It can, however, be a result of software issues, and it is a good idea to flash the Raspberry Pi with the latest software for the corresponding model.

- **2 Flashes:** Two flashes are also a result of SD card read problems. You can solve this problem by formatting the SD card and reinstalling the Operating System.

- **3 Flashes:** Indicates a `start.elf` not found issue.

- **4 Flashes:** Indicates a `start.elf` not launched issue

- **7 Flashes:** Indicates a kernel image file not found

- **8 Flashes**: SDRAM not recognized. Install a new `bootcode.bin/start.elf` firmware

Unresponsive Key presses

The leading cause of this problem is an inadequate power supply. Power your Raspberry Pi using a suitable power supply and a good power cable. Cheap cables that work with mobile phones cannot power the Raspberry Pi fully.

To fix this problem, use the recommended power supply for the Raspberry Pi and ensure the provided keyboard does not exceed the Raspberry Pi USB hub power limit of 100mA.

Keyboard & Mouse Wi-Fi Interruptions

Connecting Bluetooth and wireless powered keyboard or mouse while a USB-Wi-Fi device remains connected may cause interference between one or both of the devices. This issue is usually a result of interruptions between the 2.4 GHz frequency band between the keyboard or mouse transmitting data and the Wi-Fi dongle.

You can solve this problem by changing the broadcast channel on the access point.

Since the Raspberry Pi has a very vibrant user-base and development team, you are unlikely to encounter a problem that you cannot solve with thorough research on the internet.

In the next section, we shall look at how to use the Raspberry Pi 4 to set up innovative projects:

Section 9

Innovative Raspberry Pi Projects

You now know how to set up and get the Raspberry Pi working. In this section, we shall discuss various things you can create and the different fun ways in which you can use your Raspberry Pi.

We will start by creating simple projects that do not require additional hardware and then move on to complex projects.

NOTE: These are example projects; their purpose is to act as an illustration of what the Raspberry Pi can do once you start using it. Do not use the Pi to implement a project that will harm your device. Matter of fact, as you experiment and create new projects on your Pi, be mindful of the nature of the projects and error on the side of caution.

#: Apache & FTP Server Project

The first project we are going to look at is an Apache Web server and an FTP server. If you are familiar with Linux and how to set up Apache, feel free to skip to the next project; otherwise, stick around.

To create this project, you do not require additional software except Raspbian OS or any other Linux distribution. It is better to work with Ubuntu or other Debian based Linux distributions.

Step 1

The first step is installing Apache using the Advanced Package Manager for Debian-based distributions. It is available within the Debian repositories. Start by launching the terminal and entering the command:

```
sudo apt-get update && sudo apt-get install
apache2
```

Step 2

The next step is to install and configure a firewall. This step is optional but highly recommended. Enter the command

```
sudo apt-get install ufw
```

Step 3

Enable the firewall by executing the commands `sudo ufw enable` in the terminal. To view applications allowed or blocked applications, use the command `sudo ufw app list`

Step 4

Next, we need to give apache the ability to allow unencrypted traffic on port 80. Enter the command `sudo ufw enable`

'Apache' and verify the changes using the commands `sudo ufw status`

Step 5

The next step is to start Apache. Start by executing the command `sudo systemctl status apache2` to verify that Apache is running.

```
• apache2.service - The Apache HTTP Server
   Loaded: loaded (/lib/systemd/system/apache2.service; enabled; vendor preset: enabled)
   Drop-In: /lib/systemd/system/apache2.service.d
            └─apache2-systemd.conf
   Active: active (running) since Tue 2018-04-24 20:14:39 UTC; 9min ago
 Main PID: 2583 (apache2)
    Tasks: 55 (limit: 1153)
   CGroup: /system.slice/apache2.service
           ├─2583 /usr/sbin/apache2 -k start
           ├─2585 /usr/sbin/apache2 -k start
           └─2586 /usr/sbin/apache2 -k start
```

Step 6

If it is not running, you can start Apache by running `sudo systemctl start apache2.service`

Step 7

Once Apache is running, you can access it by opening the link

http://localhost

Read the Apache documentation to learn how to set up your local website using Apache.

Setting up an FTP Server

File Transfer Protocol (FTP) is a prevalent network protocol used to transfer files between devices connected to a network. Although the use of FTP is not as common as it was once, having an FTP server where you can upload and download files quickly is very efficient for daily work.

In this project, we are going to use vsftpd, a modern ftp service optimized for performance, stability and security to setup our server. It is important to note that you can access this server only if you are on the same network and that you require advanced settings such as port forwarding to access it outside the local network.

Step 1

The first step is to start updating the software repositories and installing vsftpd. To begin the installation, open the terminal and enter the commands

```
sudo apt-get update && sudo apt-get install vsftpd -y
```

Step 2

The second step is to set up a new configuration file for FTP and backup the original copy so that you can restore it if something goes wrong. Execute the following command in the terminal.

```
sudo cp /etc/vsftpd.conf /etc/vsftpd.conf.backup
```

Step 3

The next step is the firewall configurations. If you are not using a firewall, you can skip this step or use your package manager to install `ufw`. Enter the command `sudo ufw status` to check the current firewall status.

Step 4

Check the firewall to see if vsftp is allowed. If you do not find it, enter the following commands to add it.

```
sudo ufw allow 20/tcp

sudo ufw allow 21/tcp

sudo ufw allow 40000:50000/tcp

sudo ufw allow 990/tcp
```

Step 5

Now you can use the commands ufw status to check if the firewall allows FTP. The output should be similar to:

```
Output

Status: active


To                      Action      From

--                      ------      ----

OpenSSH                 ALLOW       Anywhere

990/tcp                 ALLOW       Anywhere

20/tcp                  ALLOW       Anywhere

21/tcp                  ALLOW       Anywhere

40000:50000/tcp         ALLOW       Anywhere

OpenSSH (v6)            ALLOW       Anywhere (v6)

20/tcp (v6)             ALLOW       Anywhere (v6)

21/tcp (v6)             ALLOW       Anywhere (v6)

990/tcp (v6)            ALLOW       Anywhere (v6)

40000:50000/tcp (v6)    ALLOW       Anywhere (v6)
```

Step 6

Once you have all the firewall configurations set up, you can then set up FTP users and the allowed directories. FTP is more secure when limited to specific directories with different permissions.

Step 7

In this next step, we are going to create a test user with the username raspbian. Enter the command `sudo adduser raspbian`. Follow through to fill the details for user creation. You can skip them as they do not affect the process of the FTP server setup.

Step 8

In this step, we are going to create an FTP directory for the associated user will the appropriate permissions.

Enter the command `sudo mkdir /home/raspbian/ftp` and set the ownership using the command `sudo chown nobody:nogroup /home/raspbian/ftp`

NOTE: If you are familiar with Linux, you can perform various permission changes to the directories. If not, leave it Be.

Step 9

This step involves editing the FTP configuration file to add users and their respective directories. Using the terminal, enter the commands `sudo nano /etc/vsftpd.conf`

Step 10

In the configuration file, uncomment the `#write_enable` to YES and `chroot_local_user` to YES. These two commands allow the user to upload files and restrict users from accessing commands or directories outside the local directory.

Step 11

To allow other users that we may configure later, add the following lines to the configuration file.

```
user_sub_token=$USER

local_root=/home/$USER/ftp
```

Step 12

The last step involves adding users to the user configuration file. Use the command echo to append the username as:

```
echo     "raspbian"    |    sudo    tee    -a
/etc/vsftpd.userlist
```

Step 13

Restart the FTP server by running the command

```
sudo systemctl start vsftpd
```

To connect to FTP, open the terminal or command prompt and enter the command `ftp <raspberry pi IP address>`. Enter the username `raspbian` and leave the password empty.

NOTE: If you are considering using the ftp service outside the local network, ensure you encrypt the connections using SSL. Follow the link below to setup SSL on vsftpd.

https://do.co/30yi4GB

#: Network Attached Storage – Home Cloud

The next project on the List is RAID Network Attached Storage, a home cloud.

If you have a lot of content available on local hard drives, you can make these files accessible throughout your local network using a NAS configured to use RAID. These are the items required for this project.

- Raspberry Pi; ideally, you should use a 4GB Raspberry Pi 4 Model.

- External Hard Drives or USB drives

- Network connection; an ethernet connection is ideal.

For this setup, we shall use RAID.

If you are not familiar with RAID configuration, check out the link below for more information.

http://bit.ly/30sqsaj

Feel free to use any other method that offers a balance between redundancy and speed.

Step 1

Ensure you update the software repositories and enter the commands: `sudo apt-get install mdadm -y`

Step 2

The next step is to format the devices in NTFS. We shall not cover formatting for each OS.

For Linux, Open Disk Utility or Gparted and create a new partition. Next, click format/Create Filesystem and select NTFS. Now click format and confirm to complete the process.

Step 3

Once you have formatted the drives, connect to the Raspberry Pi.

Step 4

Once connected, use `fdisk` or `blkid` to locate the devices and confirm that the Pi has connected to the devices and that they are working. Ensure you determine the respective devices mount points.

Example: */dev/sda1, /dev/sdb2, /dev/sdc3*

Check out the manual pages for `fdisk` and `blkid` for more information.

Step 5

Once you have chosen the RAID level to configure your devices, and then follow the next steps.

Enter the command to set up the drives into a high-performance RAID array configuration. Replace the argument `--raid-devices=X` with the number of drives connected to the Raspberry Pi, and `/dev/sda1 /dev/sdb2` with the respective mount points for the connected drives.

```
sudo  mdadm  --create  --verbose  /dev/md0  --
level=stripe      --raid-devices=4      /dev/sda1
/dev/sdb1
```

Step 6

You can confirm the RAID configuration by running the command cat /proc/mdstat

Step 7

Next, save your RAID configuration using the command:

```
mdadm --detail --scan >> /etc/mdadm/mdadm.conf
```

Step 8

The next step is to create a filesystem using the command

```
mkfs.ext4 -v -m .1 -b 4096 -E stride=32,stripe-width=64
/</dev/md0>
```

Step 9

Now mount the filesystem using the command:

```
sudo mount /dev/md0 /mnt
```

NOTE: You can configure the devices you want mounted at boot by editing the `fstab`. Using `blkid`, get the `uuid` of the md0 devices and enter the command

```
sudo nano /etc/fstab
```

Now enter the following lines at the bottom of the file, replace the uuid with your uuid from blkid.

```
UUID=2a8456d7-6fea-eba2-7728-ebd20aa238e5
/mnt ext4 defaults 0 0
```

Step 10

Once we have configured the device, we can install samba to allow file sharing. Enter the following command to install samba.

```
sudo apt-get install samba-common-bin samba -
y
```

Step 11

Once you have installed samba, add a user and share password by running the commands:

```
sudo samba -i
```

```
Step 12
```

Proceed to the next step to edit the configuration file. Enter the command `sudo nano /etc/samba/smb.conf` and add the following lines at the bottom of the file.

```
[NAS]

path = /mnt

comment = Raspberry Pi Home Cloud

valid users = pi

writable = yes

browsable = yes

Step 13
```

The last step is to restart samba by executing the command:

```
Sudo service samba restart
```

Step 14

Connect to the NAS by opening the file manager and opening network. Select the Raspberry Pi hostname and connect.

#: Amazon Echo Alexa Clone

The Amazon Echo and its voice assistant, called Alexa, is an ideal device/service for home use. It allows you to use your voice to play music and podcasts, set timers, create alerts based on specified criteria, control some home appliances, and more.

Unfortunately, the Echo can be expensive with a price range of $50-$200 dollars. The good news is that you can use the Raspberry Pi to create a personal voice assistant similar to Alexa —an Alexa clone— all without rendering the Raspberry Pi useless.

In this project, we are going to create an Alexa clone using our Raspberry Pi. In the end, you will have a device capable of completing activities such as setting timers, reading kindle books, checking the weather, setting schedules, playing podcasts and music, and other such tasks —the sky is the limit. We will also configure the clone to use the Mobile app to modify the settings with the same configurations as the real Amazon Alexa.

This project will require us to have a Raspberry Pi as expected and other additions. Below is a list of the things you will need.

- Raspberry Pi

- Micro USB cable

- USB Microphone

- Speakers

- SD card as the storage for the Raspberry Pi

- Access to the Raspberry Pi via VNC or SSH

This process will involve using the Amazon Alexa skills code and installing it on the Raspberry Pi. This project's only drawback is that it will require you to start Alexa service manually after every boot. While this can be annoying, the cost-saving —for buying a new echo— offset the small trouble of starting your voice assistant at every boot.

Here is how to create this project:

Step 1

The first step involves creating an Amazon developer account. Open the browser and navigate to the page below and create an account.

https://developer.amazon.com/

Amazon Developer Services and Technologies

amazon alexa

Alexa

Build natural voice experiences that offer customers a more intuitive way to interact with technology

amazon appstore

Amazon Appstore

Develop Android apps and games for Amazon Fire TV, Fire tablet, and mobile platforms

amazon dash
services

Dash Services

Build Amazon reordering experiences into your devices

aws

AWS Developer Center

Find tools, documentation, and sample code to build applications in your favorite language

Step 2

Once you have your developer account, navigate to the console and select the Alexa Tab

Step 3

Next, select Register a product type and then choose Alexa. Give your device a name followed by the device type.

Step 4

On the Security profile section, select 'create new profile' and add a description under the 'generals tab.' Ensure you copy the generated credentials such as Product ID, Client ID, and Client Secret.

Step 5

Under Web settings, click edit under the profile dropdown option.

Step 6

Under Allowed Origins, select add another and enter the URL

http://127.0.0.1:3000.

Add another entry and add

http://127.0.0.1:3000/authresponse

Step 7

Once the developer account completes setting and the Raspberry Pi Alexa clone profile complete setting up, it is time to build the device

Step 8

Boot up the Raspberry Pi with every required device connected. You can use PIXEL or SSH.

Step 9

Once in the terminal, navigate to your home directory and enter the command `mkdir alexa` and then navigate into the directory using the command `cd alexa`

Step 10

Once in the directory head, enter the command below to copy the repository available here.

http://bit.ly/38dx8vP

Step 11

Upon cloning the repository, navigate to the directory using the command:

```
cd alexa-avs-sample-app
```

Step 12

Once in the directory, open the file `automatted_install.sh` using nano text editor using the command `nano automatted_install.sh`. In the file, locate the client ID, Product ID, and Client secret and replace them with your credentials acquired above.

Step 13

Save the file by pressing CTRL + X followed by Y.

Step 14

List all the files in the directory to view the permissions and owners using the command `ls -la`

Step 15

To make the edited script executable, enter the command `chmod +x automated_install.sh`

Step 16

To execute the file, enter the command, `./automatetd_install.sh,` and follow the installation wizard filling the details as you see fit. The process may take 20 to 40 minutes so be patient.

Step 17

Using three different terminal windows —do not close any terminal window— execute these commands consecutively.

```
cd ~/alexa/alexa-avs-sample-app/samples
```

```
cd companionService && npm start
```

These commands start the companion service and a port to communicate with Amazon. Ensure you have npm installed and working – if misconfigured, this can be a challenge for Debian distributions.

Step 18

In the second terminal windows, execute the following commands. These commands start Java and apache Maven to register the device with Amazon.

```
cd javaclient && mvn exec:exec
```

Ensure you are in the samples folder under the `alexa-avs-sample-app` directory.

Step 19

Now navigate to the javaclient folder using the command `cd javaclient` and launch maven using the command `mvn exec:exec`

Step 20

Next, authenticate the device in the window opened and do not click OK on the second popup window.

Step 21

Next, login into your Amazon developer account and look for the authentication window for your device and click okay, which will authenticate the device. Now click OK on the popup window.

Step 22

With the First and second windows still open, Open the third window to start the wake word engine that allows you to say, "Alexa" to wake up the device so that it starts listening to you. We are going to use KITT software for this configuration.

Step 23

Navigate to the samples folder and execute the following commands.

```
Cd     wakeWordAgent/src     &&     chmod     +x
wakeWordAgent && ./wakeWordAgent -e kitt_ai
```

Step 24

All done. Once the echo engine is running, test by saying, "Alexa" to hear the Listening response from your Raspberry Pi. You can start performing basic commands like asking, "When does Halloween start?"

You will repeat steps 17-24 every time you boot up. If you are familiar with bash scripting, you can create a script to automate the process. You can also configure Alexa to use Bluetooth; this project, however, does not cover that configuration. Feel free to check out other sources for Bluetooth configuration.

#: Raspberry Pi Weather Station

In this project, we are going to build a simple but fully-operational weather station using the Raspberry Pi and Sense HAT device. This station will allow us to collect environmental weather data such as humidity, barometric pressure, and temperature.

Using python, we will also create a graphical tool to display and analyze real-time collected data. For this project, we are going to use Python programming, which means to understand the concepts involved in this project, you need a basic understanding of Python.

For this project, we are going to need our Raspberry Pi model and Sense HAT available from the resource below:

https://www.raspberrypi.org/products/sense-hat/

Sense HAT is a competent device for Space projects and weather projects. It has a Gyroscope, Accelerometer, Temperature, Barometric pressure, Humidity, and Magnetic sensors.

NOTE: While using the Sense HAT device, the collected data has approximated error values of ± 4 because of the effects of the Raspberry Pi like temperature from the heating elements.

The temperature readings from the device are in degrees Celsius and you need to convert them to Fahrenheit using the formula:

$$F = \left(C * \frac{9}{5} \right) + 32$$

We will add this formula to the Python code to perform an automatic conversion.

Humidity

We can express humidity in two forms: absolute humidity, and relative humidity. We express absolute humidity as the mass of water vapor in a specific volume of air irrespective of the temperature in kilograms per cubic meter (kg/m^3). On the other hand, we express relative humidity as the current water vapor in direct relation to the maximum possible amount at a given temperature in percentage. Sense HAT records relative humidity since it has a temperature sensor that is useful for weather forecasting.

We define barometric pressure as the weight of air at a given point. We also call it atmospheric pressure measured in atmospheres (atm) or pascals. We can express it in other units such as mmHg, hPa. You can find more information from the resource page below:

https://en.wikipedia.org/wiki/Atmospheric_pressure

Here is how to go about it:

Boot up the Raspberry Pi and open the terminal. Download the sense-hat package or clone the repository. Use the command `sudo apt-get update && sudo apt-get install sense-hat -y`

Next, create a directory on the desktop called WeatherStation. Ensure you have python3 installed and working properly. Using your favorite Python IDE, create a file inside the directory called data.py and enter the code as shown below.

```python
from sense_hat import SenseHat as sh
from time import sleep
# sense object
sense = sh()

while True:
    #get pressure data
    atm_pressure = sense.pressure()
    atm_pressure = str(round(atm_pressure, 2))
    print("Atm Pressure: ", atm_pressure, "atm\n")

    # read temperature data
    temp = sense.temperature()
    temp = str(round(temp, 2))
    print("Temperature: ", temp, "*C\n")
    temp_fah = (temp * (9 / 5)) + 32

    # read humidity data
    hum = sense.humidity()
    hum = str(round(hum, 2))
    print("Humidity: ", hum, "%\n")

    sleep(1)
```

In the code above, we use the import the class SenseHat from the Library `sense_hat` and called it sh. In the next line, we create an object called sense as a reference to the SenseHat class. We then use the functions `pressure`, `temperature`, and `humidity` to get the readings quickly. We have used the round `function` to truncate the result into two decimal places.

Conclusion

Thank you for reading this guide. I hope that you found it extremely educational and easy to implement.

I'd like your feedback. If you are happy with this book, please leave a review on Amazon.

Please leave a review for this book on Amazon by visiting the page below:

https://amzn.to/2VMR5qr

Your Gift

Let me help you master this and other programming languages quickly.

Visit

https://bit.ly/codetutorials

To Find Out More

---

[1]   https://www.shutterstock.com/image-vector/raspberry-pi-top-view-illustration-260nw-1604969923.jpg

[2]   https://www.shutterstock.com/image-photo/kiev-ukraine-august-13th-2020-microsd-1803539176?utm_campaign=image&utm_medium=googleimages&utm_source=iptc

[3]   https://media.gettyimages.com/id/161617229/photo/detail-of-hands-inserting-an-ethernet-cable-into-a-raspberry-pi-model-b-single-board-computer.jpg?s=612x612&w=gi&k=20&c=9yfPennO7qiT8bL5nkgyDhZXrWxohTScv_Sv6OU2zkw=

[4]   https://www.shutterstock.com/image-photo/single-board-credit-card-size-computer-1620029107?utm_campaign=image&utm_medium=googleimages&utm_source=iptc

---

5   https://www.shutterstock.com/image-photo/digital-camera-lens-ip-security-260nw-2126112242.jpg

www.ingramcontent.com/pod-product-compliance
Lightning Source LLC
Chambersburg PA
CBHW030659220526
45463CB00005B/1848